DATE DUE			

Life During the Great Civilizations

The Byzantine Empire

The Byzantine Empire

Don Nardo

BLACKBIRCH PRESS

An imprint of Thomson Gale, a part of The Thomson Corporation

THOMSON
GALE

Detroit • New York • San Francisco • San Diego • New Haven, Conn. • Waterville, Maine • London • Munich

© 2005 Thomson Gale, a part of the Thomson Corporation.

Thomson and Star Logo are trademarks and Gale and Blackbirch Press are registered trademarks used herein under license.

For more information, contact
Blackbirch Press
27500 Drake Rd.
Farmington Hills, MI 48331-3535
Or you can visit our Internet site at http://www.gale.com

Photo credits: see page 47.

LIBRARY OF CONGRESS CATALOGING-IN-PUBLICATION DATA

Nardo, Don, 1947–
   The Byzantine Empire / By Don Nardo.
      p. cm. — (Life during the great civilizations)
   Includes bibliographical references and index.
   ISBN 1-4103-0586-4 (alk. paper)
   1. Byzantine Empire—Social life and customs—Juvenile literature. 2. Byzantine Empire—Civilization—Juvenile literature. I. Title. II. Series.

   DF521.N37 2005
   949.5'02—dc22   2005000160

Printed in United States
10 9 8 7 6 5 4 3 2 1

Contents

Rome's Illustrious Successor

The civilization referred to today as the Byzantine Empire was not known by that name in its own time. The term *Byzantine Empire* was first used many centuries later by an eighteenth-century French historian. The people now known as the Byzantines called themselves by the Greek word *Rhomaioi* meaning "Romans." And to them, their realm was Basileia Romaion, or the "Kingdom of the Romans."

These names linking the Byzantines to ancient Rome were no mere boasts, for the Byzantine Empire emerged from the Roman Empire. To be more exact, the Byzantine realm developed from the eastern section of the Roman Empire. The western portion of that empire, with its major city of Rome (in Italy), disintegrated in the fifth and sixth centuries A.D., overrun by invaders from central and northern Europe. But the eastern portion of the realm survived. Its main city, Constantinople, meaning "City of Constantine," situated near the southern shore of the Black Sea, had been dedicated in 330 by the emperor Constantine I. At the time, eastern Rome was not yet a separate nation or empire. In fact, Constantine was sole emperor of the combined western and eastern portions of the empire. Yet for convenience, most modern historians assign that date—A.D. 330—as the start of the Byzantine realm.

Opposite Page: The Byzantine Empire began as the eastern half of the Roman Empire. This painting shows Constantinople as a bustling city.

After western Rome's decline and fall the eastern emperors tried to win back some of the lost western lands. For a while they were successful, but eventually these regions were lost once more. From then on the Byzantines, who spoke Greek (rather than Latin, the main language of western Rome), concentrated on holding together their eastern power base, centered in Greece and Asia Minor (what is now Turkey). This was no easy task, as they were almost constantly under attack from one quarter or another. Slavic tribes threatened from the north. The Persians (from what are now Iraq and Iran) assaulted Byzantine holdings in Egypt and Syria. And in the 600s Arab armies swept through the Middle East, becoming a potent new enemy.

Byzantine fortunes ebbed and flowed as these and other groups threatened the stability of the realm, whose borders and size changed frequently. Yet the Byzantine Empire weathered these storms for many centuries. All the while its emperors, religious leaders, artisans, and scribes maintained a splendid and sophisticated culture. Their architecture, paintings, mosaics, works of gold and silver, and literature were among the finest in the world. Byzantine merchants traded a broad

Byzantine society was sophisticated and complex. Its artists created jewelry like this black pearl necklace and medallions.

range of goods far and wide, making the members of the upper classes rich and comfortable. And hundreds of churches sprang up, where the devout inhabitants practiced the Eastern Orthodox version of Christianity.

Eventually, however, continued attacks on the borders, coupled with a series of weak Byzantine rulers, spelled disaster for the Byzantine Empire. A new enemy, the Ottoman Turks, hammered away relentlessly at the borders. By the early 1400s the realm had shrunk to an area of only a few hundred square miles. The end came in 1453 when the Turks managed to breach the huge defensive walls that had kept Constantinople safe for so long. The Turks, who were Muslims, renamed the city Istanbul and made Islam the official religion. After 1,123 years of pride, power, and prosperity, the last remaining vestige of the ancient Roman Empire became little more than a memory.

Ottoman Turks are shown entering the city of Constantinople in this painting. They would later rename the city Istanbul.

CHAPTER ONE

A Rigid, Class-Oriented Society

In the Byzantine Empire, far more people lacked basic freedoms and rights than enjoyed them. This is because Byzantine society was not democratic, but highly autocratic. The government was a dictatorship in which a small group of emperors and nobles wielded enormous power. They and other people of wealth and privilege were known as *honestiores*, meaning "the more honorable."

In contrast, the majority of the population consisted of various less-privileged social groups. Their members were collectively called *humiliores*, which meant "the more lowly." Some, including artisans, shopkeepers, and independent farmers, were at least free in the sense that no one legally owned them. Less fortunate were the slaves, who could be bought and sold like animals.

Whether free or not, all *humiliores* in the Byzantine realm had one thing in common —they had no say in how they were governed. Moreover, in most cases they could not better themselves by moving up the social ladder. This is because the system was rigged. Generation after generation of the *honestiores* used their wealth and position, and even passed laws, to ensure that people stayed locked in the social classes they were born into. Byzantine society was therefore very rigid and class oriented. Mere

Opposite Page: Byzantine Emperor Justinian I is surrounded by his military officers and court personnel in this mosaic.

An Emperor Aids the Downtrodden

The Byzantine government largely maintained the great social and economic divisions that separated the privileged from the poor. Yet some emperors made at least token attempts to relieve the misery of some downtrodden folk. This excerpt from the *Alexiad*, a twelfth-century book about the emperor Alexius I (reigned 1081–1118), describes a sort of combination clinic and homeless shelter he set up in Constantinople.

> All around . . . were houses for the poor and—even greater proof of his [Alexius's] humanity—dwellings for the disabled. . . . It [was] full of those who were maimed or completely incapacitated. . . . They had no land or vineyards, but each lived in his appointed house and all their needs of food and clothing were provided by the emperor's generosity. . . . The number of persons catered for in this way was incalculable [so large it could not be easily calculated].

accident of birth usually determined the amount of freedom and opportunity one enjoyed.

The Highborn and Privileged

The manner in which upper-class people benefited from the accident of their birth is well illustrated by the emperors. With a few minor exceptions, they gained their high positions through inheritance. Each emperor tried his best to leave the throne to his son or another male relative, and this resulted in a series of Byzantine royal dynasties (family lines of rulers). The dynasty founded by the emperor Justin I (reigned 518–527), for example, lasted from 518 to 610. And during the empire's height of power and prosperity—from 867 to 1057—the Macedonian Dynasty was in charge.

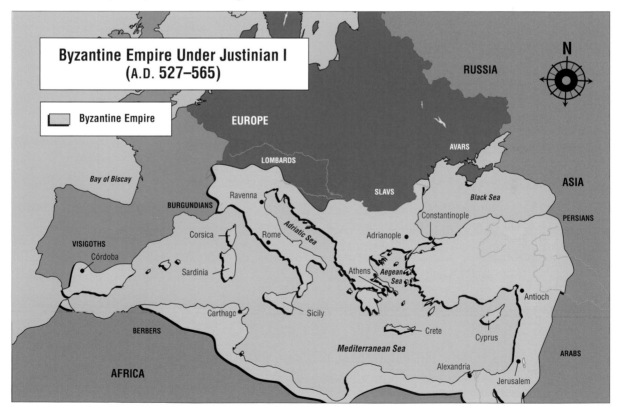

As monarchs, the emperors could do anything they pleased, at least in theory. In reality, however, their power was limited by a massive body of laws that had been largely inherited from the Roman Empire. The early Byzantine ruler Justinian I (reigned 527–565) collected the older laws and added some of his own. Most of these laws remained in effect for the remainder of Byzantine history.

Many emperors followed the law most of the time. However, some held themselves above the law when it suited them. Justinian himself was accused of corruption and misconduct by his contemporary, the Greek historian Procopius. "He was never truthful with anyone," Procopius claimed. "He was too prone to listen to accusations [against people] and too quick to punish [those people]. For he decided such cases without full examinations, naming the punishment when he had heard only the accuser's side of the matter."[1]

If the emperors were sometimes above the law, other *honestiores* routinely benefited from laws written and enforced by members of their own class. Among them were the *curiales* (rich landowners or high city officials), high-ranking military officers, and leading clergymen. All of these people enjoyed generous tax exemptions guaranteed by law. Similarly, if found guilty of a crime, they could not be whipped, tortured, or executed, as *humiliores* could. The worst penalty endured by an upper-class individual was exile or confiscation of property. In addition, *honestiores* were exempt from doing menial labor.

Urban Workers

Such labor, along with most other kinds of work, was the duty of the *humiliores*, who can be broken down into two broad groups, one urban (based in the cities), the other rural (based in the countryside). The urban working classes included craftsmen such as potters,

metalsmiths, and jewelry makers. Also among their number were shopkeepers, traveling merchants, ship captains, and bankers. These were by far the best paid and most fortunate members of the lower classes. Other urban *humiliores* had even lower social status and made less money. They included street and sewer cleaners, letter carriers, and firefighters.

A mosaic features a carpenter with a saw. Carpenters were members of the better-paid urban working class.

Although none of these workers had political rights, the law did allow them to appeal their grievances to the authorities. Each profession formed a clanlike group called a "system." Spokesmen for a system could lobby the government for various favors. They could also earn better treatment by attending rallies in the hippodrome (racetrack) and cheering for the emperor or victorious military generals.

Serfs and Slaves

Outnumbering the urban workers were the *humiliores* who lived and labored in the countryside. The rural workers were divided into two

groups—the free and unfree. Some free farmers owned their own fields and occasionally hired free laborers to help them.

But such small independent farmers were in the minority. Most could not compete with large farming estates owned by wealthy *honestiores*, who were usually absentee landlords who lived in the cities and hired others to manage their properties. In fact, the only work many rural workers could find were low-wage jobs on the big estates. Large numbers became serfs, or *coloni*, often referred to as "slaves of the soil." Legally speaking they were free. But they were completely dependent on the landowners, who protected them and allowed them to keep a small portion of the food they produced. So these workers were not much better off than slaves.

At least an owner could not sell a *colonus*. In contrast, he could sell or buy a slave. Because of the large numbers of serfs in the

Serfs work in a vineyard on an estate. Peasants earned low wages and were only a step above slaves.

17

This relief shows two slaves working an olive press. Domestic slaves were much better off than other slaves.

Byzantine realm, relatively few slaves worked on farms. Most slaves toiled in mines or worked in urban shops and the households of the well-to-do. The mine workers did backbreaking work and lived short, miserable lives. But those slaves lucky enough to work in homes often led more comfortable lives. Many of these domestic slaves received a small allowance, called the *peculium*, with which they could buy extra food or creature comforts. A few even saved up enough to buy their freedom.

Even fewer slaves chose a more radical route to freedom—escape. This was because there was basically nowhere for a runaway slave to hide for any length of time. Sooner or later someone was bound to spot him or her and alert the authorities. "Any person whatsoever who apprehends a runaway slave has an obligation to produce him in public," one law stated. Furthermore, penalties were harsh, both for the fugitive and anyone who helped him or her. According to law, "Anyone who has hidden a runaway slave is guilty of theft."[2]

Such laws made up only a small part of the larger and very strict social and legal system run by the Byzantine ruling classes. This system was designed to keep the "inferior" workers in line and maintain the wealth and high positions of the aristocrats. Largely successful, it contributed to the longevity of the empire, which lasted more than a thousand years.

CHAPTER TWO

The Refuge of Home and Family

In ancient Greece and Rome, the home and family had always been the most basic units of society. It was in the home that people were born and nurtured, and where their personalities and outlooks on life were formed. Also, many people received part or all of their education in the home. In addition, home and family were comforting refuges to fall back on in difficult or stressful times or in sickness or old age. As an extension of Greco-Roman society, Byzantine society emphasized the crucial importance of home as a place of nurturing, healing, and refuge. Whether rich or poor, people felt extremely close ties to their families and homes.

Varied Living Accommodations

From a physical standpoint, there was no typical Byzantine house (*oikia*). The size, layout, and quality of Byzantine houses varied widely depending on the status and income of the family. Members of the upper classes dwelled in large, comfortable townhouses in the cities or villas in the countryside. Most of these followed the traditional Greco-Roman courtyard plan. It consisted of several rooms, often on two stories, grouped around a central courtyard. The courtyard was roofless to take advantage of natural light in the daytime. Often it featured small gardens, cisterns

Opposite Page: Byzantine houses came in a variety of styles and sizes. Most interiors used a Greco-Roman courtyard plan.

(basins to capture rainwater), and a small altar where the family conducted home worship.

The homes of the wealthy were well furnished and cozy. Their brick or plaster walls were covered with tapestries, mosaics, and/or paintings. Each room had finely made wooden furniture, including large wooden chests for storage (because there were no closets), as well as carpets and cushions for comfort. The better homes also had bathrooms equipped with toilets and pipes (made of baked clay) to carry away sewage. Other pipes brought in freshwater from the closest aqueduct.

Middle-class *humiliores*—shopkeepers, bankers, and other professionals—who had modest incomes, often lived in similar houses. The difference was that these dwellings were usually a good deal smaller and more sparsely decorated than those of the rich. Also, few middle-class homes had elaborate plumbing. The residents had to use buckets to carry water in and sewage out.

Poor laborers and farmers, who made up the largest sector of the population, were not nearly as fortunate in their living accommodations. In the cities, the majority lived in small apartments stacked in crowded tenement blocks. These slums were usually

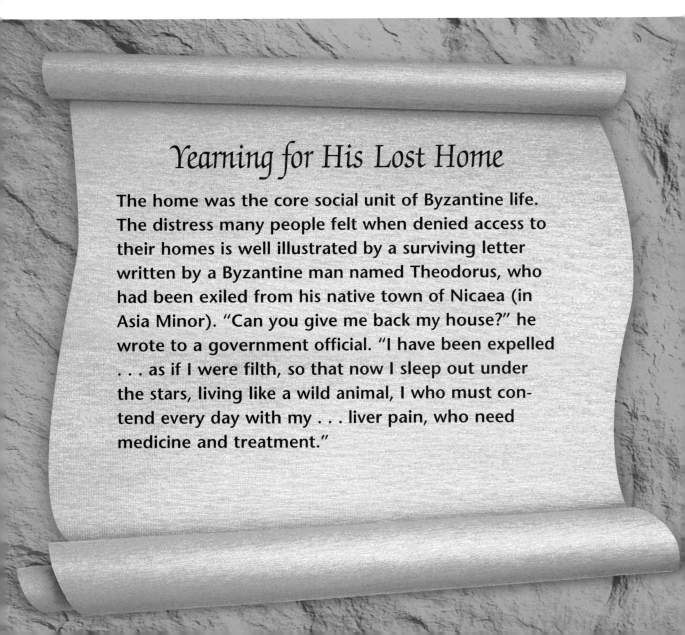

Yearning for His Lost Home

The home was the core social unit of Byzantine life. The distress many people felt when denied access to their homes is well illustrated by a surviving letter written by a Byzantine man named Theodorus, who had been exiled from his native town of Nicaea (in Asia Minor). "Can you give me back my house?" he wrote to a government official. "I have been expelled . . . as if I were filth, so that now I sleep out under the stars, living like a wild animal, I who must contend every day with my . . . liver pain, who need medicine and treatment."

poorly constructed and prone to fires and physical collapse. These neighborhoods also had high crime rates. A typical apartment had one or two rooms and no bathing or cooking facilities. In the countryside, poor farmers and laborers lived in tiny shacks made of wood or thatch (interwoven tree branches) with dirt floors. At least they had roofs over their heads. There were also large numbers of homeless people who slept in the open and sustained themselves by begging and stealing.

Family and the Position of Women

Within most homes, whether imposing or humble, dwelled a family (*oikos*). Most Byzantine families were extended. That is, they included not only the nuclear family common today—a father, mother, and their children—but also grandparents, aunts, uncles, and cousins. In some households, servants and slaves were thought of as family members, too. Such large family units had the advantage of providing extra nurturing and protection for all the members. Large families also shared household chores. Each member contributed something in the way of income, upkeep, cooking, cleaning, and running errands.

The head of the household was almost always male because Byzantine society was patriarchal (male dominated). The father (or grown son or other male family head) brought in most of the family's income. He decided how the children would be educated and whom his daughters would marry. When arranging a marriage he often consulted close male relatives, including brothers and uncles, and to a lesser degree his wife and mother.

In contrast, most of the smaller family decisions and tasks fell to the women of the *oikos*. The women, sometimes with the aid of servants, cooked, cleaned, paid the bills, and raised the children. But though women's duties and responsibilities were great, their social status was not. They had no say in politics (with the exception of a handful of empresses). Upper- and middle-class women spent most of their lives in their homes, segregated from the outside world. The main reason men sheltered women this way was the fear that the family females might socialize with other men and stain the family honor. An eleventh-century document voices the concern of a typical protective father: "An unchaste [sexually active] daughter is guilty of harming not only herself but also her parents and relatives. That is why you should keep your daughters under lock and key, as if proven guilty or imprudent."[3]

The family men were even concerned about their wives and daughters when nonfamilial male visitors entered the house. At such times the women had to retire to the "women's quarters" (*gynaikeion*), usually located in the back of the house or on the second story. In contrast, women in poorer families did venture out to work or shop. Society accepted this, seeing it as unpleasant but necessary to the survival of their families.

Educating the Young

One of a woman's most important responsibilities in the home was helping to educate the children. Mothers taught their daughters how to make clothes. Those mothers who

The Byzantine man supported and ruled the family, made all important decisions, and even arranged marriages.

could read and write passed on these skills to both daughters and sons. A middle-class boy named Michael Psellus was tutored by his mother, Theodota, and as an adult wrote to her, saying: "I owe you a double debt, for not only did you bring me into the world, but you also enlightened me with the splendor of learning."[4]

When the family could afford it, boys went on to receive more formal educations. Some were taught at home by tutors hired by the family. Others attended private schools, including some located in local monasteries. A select few, mostly from rich (but occasionally middle-class) families, attended the University of Constantinople, a prestigious school funded by the government. But no matter how far a person's education went, learning always began at home, the foundation and refuge of a person's life.

CHAPTER THREE

Religious Devotion and Practices

Next to home and family, no other aspect or institution of Byzantine society affected people more profoundly than religion. People not only attended church regularly, they also paid strict attention to numerous religious rituals and objects in their everyday lives.

The Byzantines practiced what is today called Eastern Orthodox Christianity. Christianity had become the official faith of the Roman Empire in the 300s. In fact, when he established Constantinople in the 330s, Constantine made it a Christian city from the start and went on to build many churches there. Later, the emperor Justinian I erected the Hagia Sophia, the largest and most splendid church in the world, in Constantinople.

When western Rome fell apart in the fifth and sixth centuries, the Christian bishops and emperors in the east perpetuated the faith. Most people in their region spoke Greek rather than Latin, so eastern clergymen conducted the holy rituals in Greek. The emperors also had a strong role in deciding church doctrine (official beliefs and practices). This was different from western Christianity, in which the pope decided doctrine. For example, Justinian passed laws demanding that bishops and priests conduct mass and other ceremonies in specific ways. One decree stated,

> We order all bishops and priests to repeat the divine service and the prayer, when baptism is performed, not in an undertone, but in a loud voice which can be heard by the faithful people, in such a way that the . . . listeners may be induced to . . . a higher appreciation of the praises and blessings of God.[5]

Religious Rites of Passage

The ritual mentioned in this law—baptism—was only one of many that accompanied important rites of passage in everyday life. In Christian worship, baptism is the application of water to a baby (or sometimes an older person) to initiate him or her into the church. Virtually all Byzantine babies were baptized shortly after birth. A priest immersed a child in a basin of holy water three times. Then, the baby's relatives and their friends lit candles and sang hymns as they carried the child through the streets toward home.

The Byzantine rite of baptism was performed in baptismal fonts such as this one, decorated with marble and mosaics.

29

The Most Splendid Church

The Byzantines had many churches. But for them the main focus of religious ceremony was the cathedral of Hagia Sophia, erected by the emperor Justinian I. His contemporary, the historian Procopius, describes it with a sense of wonder in his book *Buildings*.

> The church has become a spectacle of marvelous beauty, overwhelming to those who see it. . . . For it soars to a height to match the sky and . . . looks down upon the remainder of the city, adoring it . . . and dominating it. . . . The whole ceiling is overlaid with pure gold, which adds glory to the beauty, yet the light reflected from the stones prevails, shining out in rivalry with the gold. . . . Who could recount the beauty of the columns and the stones with which the church is adorned? One might imagine that he had come upon a meadow with its flowers in full bloom. . . . And whenever one enters the church to pray, he understands at once that it is not by any human power or skill, but by the influence of God, that this work has been so finely [made].

Another important religious rite of passage was marriage. All weddings took place in a church. The groom and his bride, who wore a veil over her face to keep strangers from seeing her, approached the priest. He recited holy words as the two exchanged rings and donned small crowns. (Rich people had crowns of metal and jewels. The poor made do with cheaper materials.) After the ceremony the wedding guests marched through the streets to music supplied by musicians. When they reached the groom's house, the bride finally removed her veil and everyone enjoyed a feast.

Not surprisingly, religion played a key role in the grimmest rite of passage in people's lives—their funerals. Typically, the women of a family carefully prepared the body of the deceased for burial, dressing

This is an interior view of the Hagia Sophia, the most important Byzantine church. Today it is a museum.

it in fine clothes. Then they displayed the corpse on a couch in the home, making sure that it faced southeast, toward the holy city of Jerusalem. A priest said holy words over the body as relatives and friends sang hymns. These gestures were intended to protect the dead person's soul from evil demons that might try to snatch it. Finally, the mourners carried the body to the cemetery and buried it amid more prayers and holy words.

The Ritual of Prayer

Funerals were not the only occasions on which people said prayers. People often recited them daily, both inside and outside of church.

Probably the most common prayer in Byzantine society was the "Jesus Prayer," also referred to as the "Prayer of the Heart." The exact words could vary somewhat, but always approximated these: "Lord Jesus Christ, Son of God, have mercy on me, the sinner." A person usually repeated these words over and over, sometimes for an hour or more, in the process frequently making the sign of the cross. He or she hoped that God would hear the prayer and forgive any sins recently committed.

But prayer was not always a private matter. An eleventh-century document describes a Byzantine emperor calling his entire army to pray in unison for victory in an impending battle: "When the Sun set below the horizon, one could see the heavens lit up, not with the light of [only] one Sun . . . for everyone lit torches [to attract God's attention]. . . . The prayers offered up by the army no doubt reached the very vault of heaven."[6]

Other Religious Rituals and Objects

No less important among the religious rituals was taking the Eucharist, or holy communion. In this sacred act, practiced by both eastern and western Christians, people consume a small amount of bread and wine provided by a priest. The bread represents Christ's body, the wine his blood. The ritual is intended to unify the worshipper with Christ.

During the ritual of the Eucharist, this chalice held the sacred wine, representing the blood of Christ.

In Byzantine churches, a priest took the bread and wine to the altar and recited some holy words. The altar was hidden from the worshippers by a decorated screen called the *iconostasis*. Stepping through an opening in the screen, the priest called on the faithful to approach and take communion. Many answered this call. But the elaborate setting and the priest's dramatic tone frightened some people so much that they remained cowering in their seats.

Other important rituals included the burning of incense, fasting, and almsgiving. Priests and other people burned incense during various ceremonies as well as during regular prayer, believing that its scent pleased God. To show their devotion to God, most people fasted, or refrained from eating, at certain times during the year. The most important fasting period was Great Lent, consisting of the forty days leading up to Easter. The church also urged people to give alms, or charity, to the poor.

Finally, all people respected, and sometimes prayed to, icons. These were images of holy people and events, including paintings, figurines, jewelry, and many other objects. Like the other religious aspects of everyday life, these images made the devoutly religious Byzantines feel closer to God.

CHAPTER FOUR

Byzantine Military Technology

To maintain the security of their empire for so many centuries, the Byzantines relied on a powerful military machine. It consisted in part of a strong, well-organized, and efficient army. By the mid-ninth century, nearly a hundred thousand Byzantine soldiers were in arms at any given time. This huge standing army dwarfed the tiny forces fielded by the small western European kingdoms then in existence. About four-fifths of the Byzantine troops were infantry (foot soldiers). The rest were cavalry (mounted fighters). These heavily armored horsemen, called *cataphracts*, were the pride of the army and launched devastating charges on enemy troops.

Supporting the Byzantine army was an impressive array of military technology and hardware. In fact, most Byzantine technical ingenuity was directed into military affairs. The core of the defenses was a series of formidable stone walls and fortresses designed to keep foreign attackers out.

Mighty Fortresses and Defensive Walls

When the western part of the Roman Empire fell to the barbarians, the eastern part was able to fend off most of the attackers. This was partly because the eastern Roman cities had large, well-defended defensive walls. The early Byzantine emperors took this lesson to heart. Realizing that many other enemies lurked beyond their borders, they

Opposite Page: Byzantine cavalry soldiers wage a fierce battle. The Byzantine Empire defended its borders with a large army.

In the top-right corner of the image:

M. *Strada di Fismatica*
N. *Strada a Constantinopoli*
O. *Porta delle Sette Torri*
Ant. Prinlay F.

S. *Contra Porta*
Sette torri che
Scariono sell

For protection, Constantinople was surrounded by fortresses and towers made of thick stone, with a moat around the complex.

strengthened the empire's existing defenses and erected many new ones. Some of the most extensive walls and fortresses were built by Justinian I in the sixth century. Describing some of the fortifications along the Danube River, on the realm's western frontier, Procopius wrote:

> Justinian bordered the river with numerous fortresses and set up guard posts along the banks to prevent the barbarians from crossing. . . . [But] he was not content . . . [with] these river forts alone, but constructed great numbers of other defense-works all over . . . until every [house and farm] was either transformed into a fortress or was protected by a nearby forti-fied position.[7]

The Byzantines inherited much of the technology to build these defenses from the Romans. But Byzantine military engineers improved upon these ideas and techniques. The stone battlements built to protect Constantinople, Nicaea, Antioch, and other Byzantine cities were immense, complicated, and a marvel to behold. When European crusaders marched past Constantinople on their way to Palestine in the twelfth century, they were amazed. Their own castles were puny by comparison. The Byzantine capital was surrounded by a defensive perimeter fourteen miles in circumference, with some four hundred colossal guard towers. Some sections of the perimeter had two mighty walls—an inner one 40 feet high and 15 feet thick, and an outer one 30 feet high. Outside these walls stretched a moat 60 feet wide and 15 to 30 feet deep. It is no wonder that Constantinople survived siege after siege during the Byzantine era.

Besides walled fortresses, the Byzantines used defense systems such as drawbridges, which could be drawn up to block entry.

Many Ingenious Devices

However, it was not simply the sheer size of these fortifications that made them successful. Byzantine engineers also incorporated many ingenious devices designed to harm attackers. One of these technological

Constantinople Falls

In the concluding section of *The Decline and Fall of the Roman Empire*, English historian Edward Gibbon captures the destruction of Constantinople's defenses at the hands of the Ottoman Turks in 1453.

> At daybreak . . . the Turks assaulted the city by sea and land. . . . The ditch [moat] was filled with the bodies of the slain; they supported the footsteps of their companions. . . . The cries of fear and of pain were drowned in the martial [warlike] music of drums [and] trumpets. . . . From the [infantry] lines, the galleys [warships], and the bridge, the Ottoman artillery thundered on all sides; and the camp and city, the Greeks and the Turks, were involved in a cloud of smoke, which could only be dispelled by the final deliverance or destruction of the Roman Empire. . . . The number of the Ottomans was fifty, perhaps a hundred, times superior to that of the Christians; the double walls were reduced by the cannon to a heap of ruins.

gimmicks was machicolation. It consisted of a stone ridge that projected outward from the top of the battlements. The builders drilled holes
in the stone through which defenders dropped big rocks or boiling oil
onto the attackers below.

Another common feature of Byzantine defensive walls was the
arrow loop, also called the "murderess." Arrow loops were narrow vertical slits cut into the walls at intervals. The safely hidden defenders
shot arrows through the slits at attacking soldiers.

Other effective defensive devices included portcullises, drawbridges, and barbicans. A portcullis was a heavy wooden gateway door
that defenders moved up and down using chains attached to a winch
located in a small chamber above the main gates. Drawbridges also
utilized winches. A drawbridge was a wooden platform that spanned
the moat and could be drawn back during an attack. Chains attached
to the outer ends of the bridge ran up to the winch, which pulled the
unit up into a vertical position. This became an added barrier that was
difficult to penetrate. Still another device that kept attackers at bay—

*Greek fire was
the Byzantines'
deadly secret
weapon. When
sprayed onto
ships, they burst
into flame.*

the barbican—consisted of an extra wall that projected outward from the main wall on one or both sides of a gate. To reach the gate, the enemy soldiers first had to move past the barbican. And as they did so, the defenders on top of the barbican showered them with a deadly rain of arrows, rocks, and other missiles.

The Frightening Greek Fire

The Byzantines were equally formidable when they went on the offensive. In addition to their well-organized infantry and horsemen, they had a secret weapon—Greek fire—which struck fear into the hearts of all who encountered it. Actually, the term *Greek fire* was coined by enemy observers. The Byzantines themselves called it "marine fire" or "liquid fire." The emperors and their inventors kept the ingredients a guarded state secret, and to this day no one knows for sure what these ingredients were. Modern scholars think this early chemical weapon was petroleum (oil) based, with additions of substances possibly including sulfur, salt, and quicklime.

Whatever it was made of, there was no question that Greek fire was a devastating weapon. Byzantine engineers heated the liquid to a certain temperature. Then soldiers loaded it into big tubes and sprayed it onto enemy ships, which immediately burst into flames. Moreover, the burning substance clung to sails, oars, decks, and sailors' clothes and skin and could not be extinguished with water.

Into the Mists of History Past

Despite their towering fortifications, large cavalry battalions, and secret weapon, the Byzantines were not invincible. In the end they fell prey to a still more deadly weapon—the cannon. In 1453 the Ottoman Turks bombarded Constantinople's walls with cannonballs continuously for 49 days and finally managed to break through them. In the words of the eighteenth-century English historian Edward Gibbon: "The Ottoman artillery thundered on all sides, and . . . the double walls were reduced by the cannon to a heap of ruins."[8]

As the city, and with it the empire, fell, the last Byzantine emperor, Constantine XI, died fighting on the battlements. His body was never found. Along with his once mighty realm, he vanished into the enveloping mists of history, the inevitable fate of all human civilizations.

Notes

Chapter 1: A Rigid, Class-Oriented Society

1. Procopius, *The Secret History*, trans. Richard Atwater. Ann Arbor: University of Michigan Press, 1961, p. 42.
2. *Justinian Digest*, quoted in Thomas Wiedemann, *Greek and Roman Slavery*. London: Croom Helm, 1981, p. 190.

Chapter 2: The Refuge of Home and Family

3. Quoted in Paul Veyne, ed., *A History of Private Life: From Pagan Rome to Byzantium*. Cambridge, MA: Harvard University Press, 1987, p. 573.
4. Michael Psellus, *Chrono Graphia*, trans. E.R.A. Sewter. New Haven, CT: Yale University Press, 1953, p. 43.

Chapter 3: Religious Devotion and Practices

5. Justinian, *Novella*, quoted in S.P. Scott, trans., *The Civil Law*, vol. 12. Cincinnati, OH: Central Trust, 1932, p. 155.
6. Quoted in John Julius Norwich, *Byzantium: The Decline and Fall*. New York: Knopf, 1996, p. 27.

Chapter 4: Byzantine Military Technology

7. Procopius, *Buildings*, quoted in Christon I. Archer et al., *World History of Warfare*. Lincoln: University of Nebraska Press, 2002, p. 119.
8. Edward Gibbon, *The Decline and Fall of the Roman Empire*, ed. David Womersley, vol. 3. New York: Penguin, 1994, pp. 960–61.

Glossary

alms: Charitable offerings.

arrow loop: In a defensive wall, a narrow slit through which to shoot arrows at attackers.

barbican: An extra wall that projects outward from the main defensive wall of a fortress, usually on one or both sides of a gate.

***cataphracts*:** Mounted, well-armored warriors.

***coloni* (singular is *colonus*):** Serfs or poor tenant farmers who were totally dependent on the rich landowners on whose estates they worked.

***curiales*:** Rich landowners or high city officials.

***gynaikeion*:** The "women's quarters" in a Greek or Byzantine home.

***honestiores*:** "The more honorable"; upper-class, privileged Byzantines.

***humiliores*:** "The more lowly"; lower-class, less privileged Byzantines, including craftsmen, shopkeepers, and menial laborers.

icon: An image or object depicting a holy person or event.

***iconostasis*:** A screen, usually beautifully decorated, to hide the altar from the congregation in a Byzantine church.

machicolation: A stone ridge that projects outward from the top of a defensive wall.

***oikia*:** A house.

***oikos*:** The family.

patriarchal: Male-dominated.

***peculium*:** A small amount of money given to slaves as a sort of allowance by their masters.

portcullis: In a fortress, a heavy wooden door that can be raised and lowered by means of a winch.

***Rhomaioi*:** "Romans"; the Greek term used by the Byzantines to describe themselves.

rural: Based in the countryside.

system: In Byzantine society, a clanlike group made up of members of one profession.

thatch: Interwoven twigs and tree branches.

urban: Based in the city.

winch: A device consisting of a cylinder with ropes or chains wound around it; when someone turns the cylinder, the ropes raise or lower whatever object they are attached to.

For More Information

Books

Isaac Asimov, *Constantinople: The Forgotten Empire*. Boston, Houghton-Mifflin, 1970.

Tracy Barrett, *Anna of Byzantium*. New York: Delacorte, 1999.

Editors of Time-Life Books, *What Life Was Like amid the Splendor and Intrigue of the Byzantine Empire, A.D. 330–1453*. New York: Time-Life, 1998.

Michael Grant, *From Rome to Byzantium*. New York: Routledge, 1998.

Vicki Leon, *Outrageous Women of the Middle Ages*. Hoboken, NJ: Wiley, 1998.

Elsa Marston, *The Byzantine Empire*. Tarrytown, NY: Benchmark, 2002.

Web Sites

The Byzantine Empire (www.newadvent.org/cathen/03096a.htm). A useful general history of the Byzantine Empire, with numerous links to extra information on related topics.

Early Byzantine Period (www.fhw.gr/chronos/08/en/k/main/frame/k3.html?2). An excellent overview of Byzantine civilization, with sections on the government, people and their social status, the church and worship, the serfs and slaves, and much more.

Eastern Orthodox Church (http://en.wikipedia.org/wiki/Byzantine_Empire). After logging onto the Wikipedia site for the Byzantine Empire, click on the link labeled "Eastern Orthodox" in midpage for an enlightening synopsis of Byzantine religious beliefs and practices. The Wikipedia site also contains a great deal of other material on the Byzantines.

Index

Picture Credits

About the Author

Historian Don Nardo has published many volumes for young readers about ancient and medieval civilizations, including *The Roman Empire, A Travel Guide to Ancient Alexandria, The Etruscans, Empires of Mesopotamia, Living in Ancient Egypt, Life on a Medieval Pilgrimage,* and *Weapons and Warfare of the Middle Ages.* He lives in Massachusetts with his wife Christine.